THAT I WOULD DREAM ABOUT IT

THAT I WOULD DREAM ABOUT IT

Poems
by
EEVA MARIA AL-KHAZAALI

Adelaide Books
New York / Lisbon
2019

THAT I WOULD DREAM ABOUT IT
Poems
By Eeva Maria al-Khazaali
This book is originally published in Finnish with the title "Että näkisin siitä unia" in Nov, 2018 by ntamo, Helsinki, Finland.

Copyright © by Eeva Maria al-Khazaali

Cover design © 2019 Adelaide Books
Author's photograph: Isabel Andersson, 2018.

Published by Adelaide Books, New York / Lisbon
adelaidebooks.org

Editor-in-Chief
Stevan V. Nikolic

All rights reserved. No part of this book may be reproduced in any manner whatsoever without written permission from the author except in the case of brief quotations embodied in critical articles and reviews.

For any information, please address Adelaide Books
at info@adelaidebooks.org
or write to:
Adelaide Books
244 Fifth Ave. Suite D27
New York, NY, 10001

ISBN-10: 1-950437-48-5
ISBN-13: 978-1-950437-48-1

Printed in the United States of America

You don't know that I am
a real person. I tell

you how we come to
the end of each other. Teach me what it is
to forgive, everything,

return back home,
to the shores of pitch black rocks.

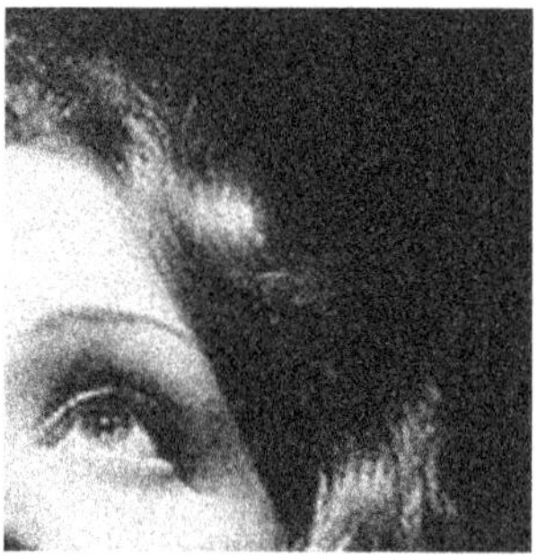

Woman: Where is your heart?
Man: Here. With you.

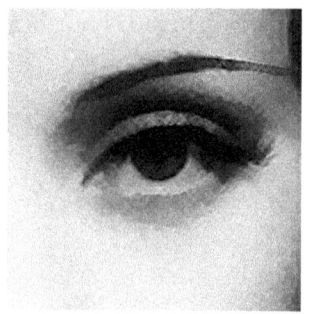

I am the woman of my life,
the only one and unforgettable.

The old man can only
in his dreams contact
his nonexistent lover.

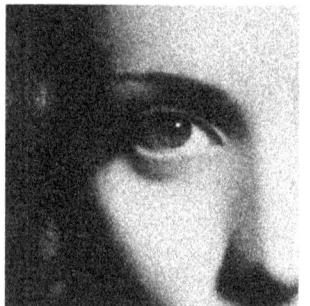

And just.
Here. The patience
is just here.

She looks at the mirror
and in the mirror
there is her back.

We are equal, still

I write to you till the end,
my end, as
I would wake up in the night only to scream your name,

this is not over, nothing is,
not a continent or an ocean
will come between us, we are still.

Once this things will not make me unhappy.
Now I have to rush, drink and be merry.
Yes, yes, say it one more time and let me fly.

What it did smell like in your room, what
did the strong tea taste like.
All this I have so soon forgotten.
How do the senses remember, and what.

A thousand years of history
in the figures of the clouds,
you woke me up.

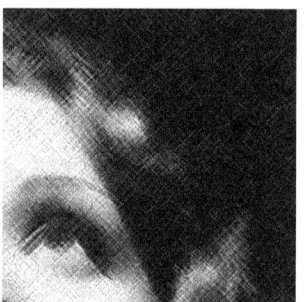

You write inside of a diamond.

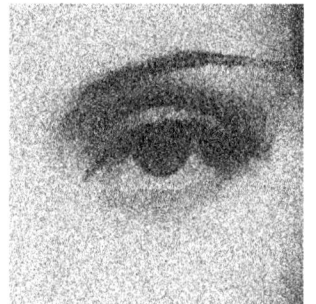

I will still do as I can.
Everything clear.
To see, to see.

A white-headed horse
comes towards me
like a vision, I listen
how the handsome animal neighs,
how its hooves slam
on the manège, fine
step patterns, now I understand
how I am able to do this,
sit alone on the edge of darkness,
hunt down the light of the white-headed horse.

in the light of the street lamps, orange nights
as this chanson, this cold bitten
moment after the sun has times ago
set on its ways, and drowned
in the clouds and the ocean, after he left
i haven't slept and how I hear
how he speaks, a gloomy
shape of a voice with trouser legs flare
in the dark of the night, in the middle of the
winter I think how soon it is spring.

Listen to the night
how it reads
the letters out loud,
keeps awake and awaits,
sets the pen on the paper
and starts scratching,
comes through the doors and windows
as the uninvited guest.

How for a moment all of this reminds and is remembered.
On a street of a metropolis as escaping a shadow.
How to think so not to destroy?

room filled of empty, with a view
   to the space of the heart.

Even that I don't think of you
is a thought of you.

The lipstick spreads over the lips,
there's a hole in the knee-high sock.
The rusted bangles
chime, reflect
the decayed paint of the house.
The bed is a cemetery of wasps.

On the street all the buttons
of my jacket fall,
one by one,
between my steps.
I find the eye of the needle
in the grass and a ball of thread.

I sew the buttons to the jacket.

I sit in the blind spot under the trees
and look at the field opening in front of me.
My silence is reforming, the theatrical gesture
of my hand, the sweetness of the berry trees.

in hundred years, in the sand lands
the coffins are not easily decayed.

You won't take this well, I know.
You press your head in your hands and sigh.

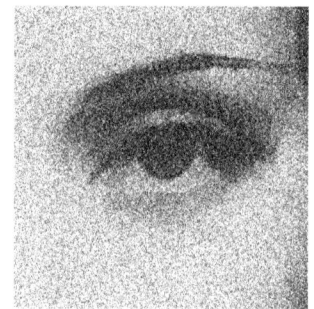

A woman in white walks before in a plain.
I cannot reach her.

This city avalanches over me.
This city pierces my heart.
This city is a body sleeping
in a dead dream beside me.

A small bird breathes in my shoulder blade
when I stay awake the night of the bare body.
    I want to hold the bird but I cannot
        I cannot crush its wings, take
            it to the lap of my fist.

the tires slip on the driveway. We speed fast.
We are on our way to a family reunion across the country.
For that she has hanged her best outfit on sight.
She wears it only once in ten years and for sure
it has not a wrinkle, so carefully she has
gone through every turn with an
iron.

She stops the car a mile before our
destination and gets dressed.
The tights won't fall apart. For that she
has prepared with plastic gloves.
She is stunning. I offer her a mint which melts
in her mouth before we park the car and
get up to the storages of the
building.

I split the apple,
I heard bones crush.
I am leaving
towards something, a small rose
shall bloom on the drawer.

Well, the apple

I sense that
an apple is clear
light green and sorrow
bites so hard that the reason
spits the seeds on the ground.

The seed sprouts, a tree grows.
The tree freezes
in the fumes of winter.

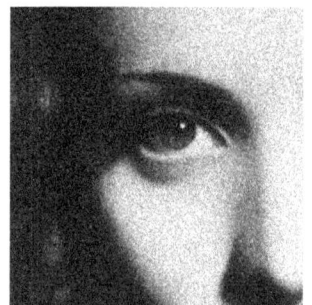

What skies did you fall from?
The stars drop on the street.
You might be coming through that door the last time.
You are a shadow left between the door.
I lost music for years
but now I found it again.
The crying isn't emptying of me,
sadness takes an another form.
You, too, alone with your sorrow.
I am no longer a time before you.

The tattooed memories still resonate in us,
knowing our names.
We let it cast this moment.

The eyes

An old film camera around the neck,
everywhere, film roll like pearls.
The eye of the whale is laying in the sand
as space written from the eyes.
So put down your glass and look directly.
She takes photographs
through the window,
she takes photographs
of the darkness outside.
In the still image still the black
wells of pupils,
the time of eyes, memories.
The shadow reveals
how the gaze sins
in the colorful ocean of irises.
I keep my eyes open
towards the world.

Do you remember my heart,
your maps?
The constellations holy above us.

The ink of a drawing pen is shying,
towards language and eternity,
life that remains after life is gone.

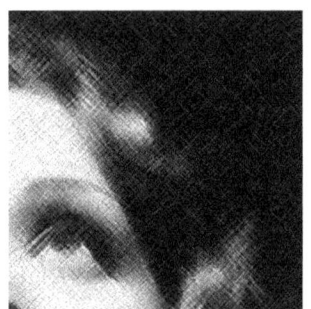

The drawing

I make a projection, search for an angle.
It spins around, slims and fattens.
I draw a lonely chair and a bird
on its back.
The wings are heavy moss as feet,
escaping further away in the horizon,
always reducing, disappearing, fading out till the end,
without reservations. Where there is a bird,
is my chair also in the end of the picture, close-by
to the place of most distance.

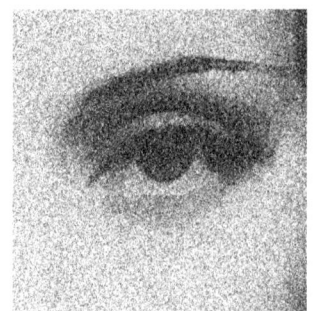

The paper white morning, opening pages of a book,
meant to be read,
the ink black letters.
I read a volume, dogear, underlining,
the whole weight of the book like a chest.

My name

I have forgotten a lot about my life:
after all my birth doesn't belong here or there,
the pitch black night of a wolf, the yellowed lace of a
wedding gown, the love letters signed with blood of a heart,
as the results of Rorschach test: the empty,

unnamed absence.
In that image the perfect history: I am
at least a thousand years old,
as painfully dull, boring as a clinical picture, the blood
sugar, milk and cigarettes, *I like milk and cigarettes*,
a soporific book from the reference library, with a biography
twirled inside: a name that one has always spelled wrong.

The pearls roll
towards the palms, a crescent moon in the heel of
the shoe, that all I have forgotten: now I confess.

I am only the decades of the pages I have written, as
a fern in the hopeless longing of the dying land.

My heart is open and my lungs are full
of the north, I don't feel it, it shakes oddly.

There's a pitch dark road so long as one can walk,
there's a road long and bruised, forest made
bluer, winter roads and moonlight, there
I come from. My body changes
from paper to flesh, I lay it down from
my lap as a strange child.

I would like to
kick the stars of the sky.

My God,
let me love.

A dream

This is a recurrent, winding,
meandering, crying dream,
twisted as pixels
turned as a warped position.
I see the shape of your name.
I have stayed awake for your name,
as a body, for a long time,
nocturnal insomniac nights when
the animals and insects crowd
outside from their shells and dens,
make a nest in my hair,
the last sign of my humanity:
its semantics, I make
this moment a shared dream.
When a dream becomes shared,
when a dream becomes a shared memory,
not only the morning frightened panorama,
I witness still myself and the fait accompli.
And why do I know when awake,
that I am seeing a sleeping dream,
my literature.
I verify this dreams memory,
I want to be sure, that the city still is.
That it is still there.

Eeva Maria al-Khazaali

That is stands there still
and not even desolate, that the same
streets are still there
where I once forgot them
and that you can see the grim
and the glitter,
and I can witness
that the citizens still
live in their city on and on.
It is not harder than this.
This is not harder than that.
The decades spread out as papers
around me, spread as papers
as butterflies that open their wings
and stardust spreads in the entire room.
Nothing is so special
that I would dream about it.
Nothing is so meaningful
that it would inevitably be followed by this moment,
a dream or its explanation.
The weight of the ribs, the pressure on the ribs,
I see dreams where I am
an another me, this woman,
a narrator, painted lips
in the mirror image.
I am not only the explanation of my dream.

THAT I WOULD DREAM ABOUT IT

Most of my life has happened
in a dream.
I see how the form of my words
is heavy, its pulse is slow
as a dying bird on the road
that I don't dare to watch,
the wings in blood and my chest open:
the heart still beats on its last
and the eyes are muted,
drop in the verses that I fix
as old clothes, I sting
the needle as a font.
My heart exists
for this.
The shreds of clouds on the sky
all are important
and significant.
I only see the simple structure
which on a night like this
makes history.
But I have also decided
that I only cry if my tears
roll upwards as an electric shock
in pouring rain, a thunder storm,
if there are cherry blossoms raining outside,

Eeva Maria al-Khazaali

if the impossible happens - that kind,
which won't happen unless in the logic of a dream,
but only when you fall asleep
in a dream that will break your lashes.
The dream feels like infinity
as does this moment that
passes painlessly, quickly.
I cannot find the platform at the railway station,
I cannot find a path or a bus connection.
I return to that city always, always
when I sleep.
The street corners fall on the cobble stones,
and the birds on the side of the plaza
fall to the cobble stones.
That city I have drowned myself into,
that city I have stayed in, partly,
partly, I am still there when I close
my eyes and always when my eyes strike open,

I miss the place,
even if my heart
becomes a wreck, a time after a time,
a verse by verse.
This dream is not special in any form.
It is not synergistic, there is no

THAT I WOULD DREAM ABOUT IT

    Pegasus flying in it or centaurs
    wandering in wildly roaring grass.
        It is possible
      that I see no other dream
        at all: only this
      English countryside:
I walk on the meadows and parks
I look for paths in the oak groves
    and I always find the same
        faceless face.
      I am crushed
    under the weight of my dream,
      under the petals,
when a girl like a cherry blossom,
    willow branch, the roots
      cutting the path.
I have found all the abandoned villages,
      deserts, waste lands, all
where to disappear without leaving a trace,
    but I won't go to disappear,
I am not looking for a place to forget,
      I want to remember:
        to live and burn
      as the city lights,
    the fire flooding the streets,

Eeva Maria al-Khazaali

I want to remember - all,
I want to be part of
the legs, arms and gateways of the city.
I dashed to cover myself from the rain
I walked barefoot as in a paradise,
I wanted to fall asleep in the noise
of the railway station,
to stay in the midst of the people,
go through everything and forgive.
I can begin again in here,
tell everything as it is:
the harbors, freeways,
trains, taxis and forest roads
leading me to this town
where I will never find myself again.
There is barbed wire on the rooftops
and satellites only in the suburbs,
and people, everyone hopes to be
somewhere else, with these coordinates I
fill my memory, my mind, I trip over
on the root, in the beginning, the city
distances itself,
and it will always be: the rocks, the shore,
the railways, taxis, the tears rolling upwards,
the petals raining on my eyes,
the silencing frightening: images,

THAT I WOULD DREAM ABOUT IT

symbols, metaphors,
they don't say anything,
I am not crying about this,
winding, meandering, falling dream,
falling like a soldier on a mission,
the statues are build for him, the grave stones,
and the parade of the soldiers has been held for him,
from this city he has also left from,
from this I cannot find and
to which I want to return to.
Wolverhampton,
you are the forgotten miracle of England.
I have feelings for that town.
I am bone, bone,
and skin, I have learned
to close up as a flower,
and I cannot find houses anymore
from the city plan,
look at the drawings of the architect,
the symmetry of the tall buildings
and the sad longing of history,
the reflection clinging to the bell tower,
glass windows and abandoned
buildings and people in them
which do not live anymore
even in our memories.

Eeva Maria al-Khazaali

What is true in this dream,
it is what is true now:
as lost in the tissues of dream,
I have been lost from the city
and its streets as
I would have dropped from the edge
of the world and wouldn't have made
on this other side,
home, in that room in the center
of the town and I wouldn't have walked
in the cherry blossom rain,
and the logical tears of the dream
won't roll in any direction
as the pearls rolling on the shore,
what do they do there,
I only have this memory:
only these memories which I open
as braided hair, for the last time,
braided as a child, tightly
so that the skin turns into paper
I am a small death
when I escape towards my memory,
as thoughts, dreams and memories return
where I am not and where I will
never return

THAT I WOULD DREAM ABOUT IT

even if all the cameras of the world
would picture every corner, all the turns of the world,
turn images, so that I would see better
where I have forgotten most of myself,
so that I would book tickets
to that town, I would travel by train
to the station, I would take my legs,
drop my hands on the ground,
collect my limbs, my memories,
my time, my dream, I would take myself
to go through my memories,
I would split them like apples,
I would let them fall from my hands like coins,
I would look directly to them:
directly as the eye of the storm,
in the thunder storm of
the cherry blossom petals,
I only find again
a dream where I lose everything,
I lose the town, its borders,
walls, windows, doors and gateways
all of the cobble stones and the pigeons
falling asleep on the cobble stones.
And I have never been over it
that the town is unattainable to me.

Eeva Maria al-Khazaali

And I have never been over it
that the town is a miniature world.
This is a confession about a dream
that I will not see, which I don't
want to see.
It has the scent of fog,
and dirt and the feel of them.
In the end it became real.
It repeats, before it is verified
that I will never find the same town,
it is an experience, memory, memory.
What is crucial are the days
the dreams were sliding
as alga on the open waters,
and I will return to the fact
I will never find my heart, my home,
my town, where I lived and studied for an year,
where I watched movies and fell asleep in the cinema,
the birds were falling asleep on the cobble stones, streets,
the town was falling.
Nothing can be undone.
That I will tell you immediately.
Nothing can be changed from what happened.
I can forget the gloom, the sad past,
memories I can forget.

THAT I WOULD DREAM ABOUT IT

I cannot let myself to that town
and say in the end nothing else that
the town as an illusion is disappearing
from the map,
it has no borders anymore, its trams
and supermarkets will stay,
the good ones walk past
the bad.
I search, I have the time to find,
familiar roundabouts,
you drive freeway M6 to it,
from that intersection you might still turn.
Only thing left from the dream
is a broken language,
dissolving to dust,
the sounds fall, the verses twist and warp
to letters.
In the end it is not about anything else:
I am in a difficult position, and forgotten
myself to this,
crooked as the verses and letters,
alternative histories all in me at the same time.
This is a possibility to interpret a dream,
what happened, the explanation of a dream, the reading.

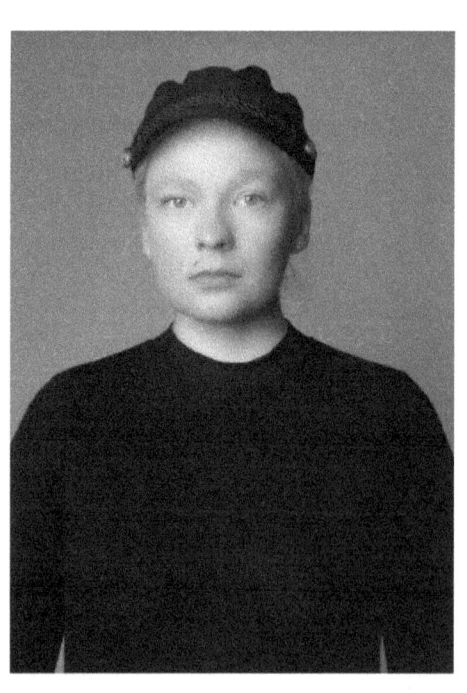

About the Author

Eeva Maria al-Khazaali (previously Eeva Karhunen) is a poet (born 29th of September, 1986 in Finland) writing about love and growing up as an artist. Even if the key narration of her work is about romantic love, she wishes to include her focus in the tradition of feminist autofiction, empowering women through her art. She is using personal experiences and encounters as her material. Each page of the book here could be dedicated to someone in the past, yet she wishes each page to speak to a different reader which represents the unknown to her, as do the dreams she finds herself in. She explains her interest in working on dreams and daydreams as in this book, "That I would dream about it" she travels through her own memories, the passing moments in time and thoughts of awakening beside her lover. This is the most private space she will ever be revealing to the world. This is her personal space she invites readers to examine. Empty spaces and light are her starting points when writing a poem. Her creative writing technique avoids addressing the intimate too rawly: instead of concrete issues about the feminist experience, she is writing in symbols and metaphors from a bodily register and rejoicing the more abstract concepts. She is obsessed about the idea of women writing history, making their own stories heard and thoughts read by those she loves and those she doesn't yet know. She is confessional yet names no-one in her works, pointing out singular events and thoughts to be relevant for the next decades or even centuries to come. In this book, Eeva Maria writes in both the aphoristic and the grandious verse, leaving her work to be seen as minimalist yet again freely flowing, without limiting or imprisoning her creative talent to a spesific form of poetry, varying from a one-verse poem to a liturgy-like ending of her book in question. Eeva Maria's interest vary in multiple fields of art, mentioning blockbuster Hollywood films as a guilty pleasure, disposable Kodak camera photography as a way of perceiving the world and the departments of fine art all over the world her truest inspirations. Eeva Maria also experiments artist mediums in her real life alongside with creative writing and poetry. She names her greatest influence to be a French author, Marguerite Duras because of the author's precise wording and expressive bravery of her sentences. Eeva Maria is active on Instagram @iameevamaria and on Twitter @eevaunen.

www.ingramcontent.com/pod-product-compliance
Lightning Source LLC
Chambersburg PA
CBHW032249080426
42735CB00008B/1067